Ronnie Barker
# Fletcher's Book
# of Rhyming Slang

illustrated by Malcolm Poynter

**Pan Original** Pan Books
London and Sydney

'Hello, me old cock!' Cock: cocksparrow = barrow: barrow of soil = boil: boil and bake = cake: cake and jam = ham: ham and pickle = tickle: tickle and touch = Dutch: Dutch plate = *mate*. Simple, isn't it?

# Contents

*Acknowledgements* I would like to acknowledge the help of all my pals among the actors and technicians during the filming of *Porridge* in remembering some of the more obscure slang terms; especially Mr Jack Towns, a man in a million.

First published 1979 by Pan Books Ltd,
Cavaye Place, London SW10 9PG
© Witzend Productions Limited 1979
ISBN 0 330 25980 6
Printed and bound in Great Britain by
Hazell Watson & Viney Ltd, Aylesbury, Bucks

# Introduction

Of course, everybody (in the nick and out of it) has heard of rhyming slang. It dates back, as horrible Ives would say, to time immoral. At least a hundred and fifty years, because the wife's mother doesn't remember it starting.

Of course, in Slade Prison it has its uses, particularly as most of the screws (sorry, prison officers) come from up here in Cumberland, and so don't understand the finer points of the cockney rhymes. However, let's be clear about one thing – this little book isn't written to help them out – no: may their socks rot. No, this is for you, to while away a pleasant hour learning something useful. I've certainly had a pleasant few hours, collecting it all up from me mates inside here. Of course, rhyming slang has always changed with the times, so there may be a few words in here that are a surprise even to seasoned slangers like Arthur Mullard and Fanny Craddock (who is herself already immortalized in slang, as representing a piece of haddock. So be careful what you ask the lady in the fish shop for).

Anyhow, I hope you consider it worth a quick *butchers* – it will give you something to *rabbit* to the *trouble* about in the *skein*, instead of having to fall back on the old *Oedipus* all the time.

Keep smiling.

Yours,

*Fletch*

# Parts of the body

| Boat | Boat Race | Face |
| Barnet | Barnet Fair | Hair |
| Errol | Errol Flynn | Chin |
| I suppose | — | Nose |
| North | North and south | Mouth |
| Minces | Mince pies | Eyes |
| Kings | King Lears | Ears |
| Uncle | Uncle Ned | Head |
| Hampsteads | Hampstead Heath | Teeth |

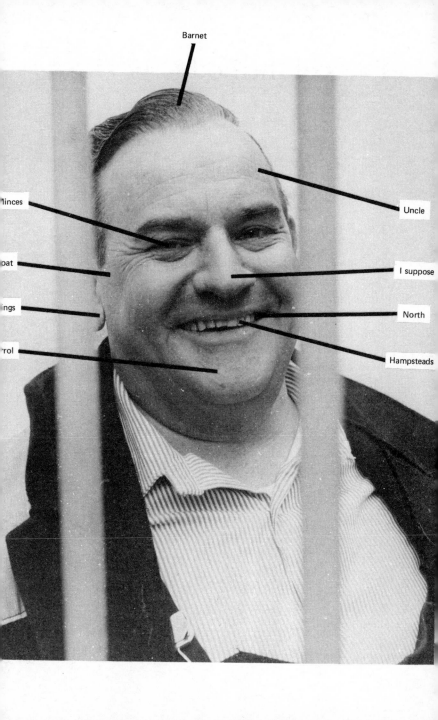

Barnet

Uncle

Minces

oat

I suppose

ings

North

rol

Hampsteads

# Parts of the body

| | | |
|---|---|---|
| Germans | German bands | Hands |
| Longers | Longers and lingers | Fingers |
| Darby | Darby Kelly | Belly |
| Jumping | Jumping Jack | Back |
| Scotches | Scotch pegs | Legs |
| Plates | Plates of meat | Feet |
| Marys | Mary Rose | Toes |
| Loaf | Loaf of bread | Head |
| Trunks | Trunks of trees | Knees |
| Chalk | Chalk Farm | Arm |
| Gregory | Gregory Peck | Neck |

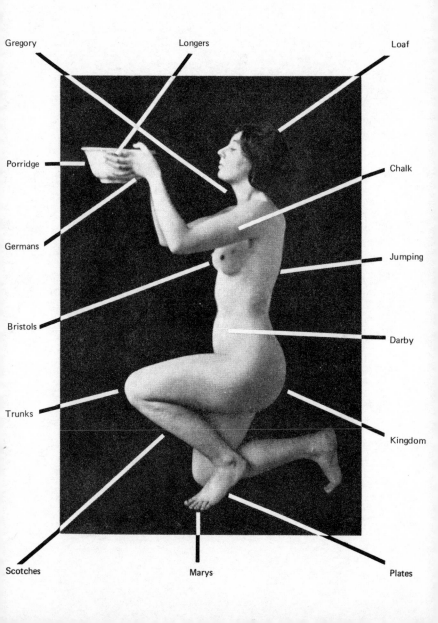

Gregory

Longers

Loaf

Porridge

Chalk

Germans

Jumping

Bristols

Darby

Trunks

Kingdom

Scotches

Marys

Plates

# Glossary

**Arm** Chalk Farm
**Army** Daft and barmy
**Aunt** Mrs Chant

**Baby** Basin of gravy
**Back** Jumping Jack
**Bad** Shepherd's plaid, or Sorry and sad
**Banana** Gertie Gitana
**Bank** Tin tank
*__Barrow__** Cock sparrow
**Bass** Begger boy's ass
**Bed** Skein of thread
**Beef** Stop thief
*__Beer__** Pig's ear
**Believe** Christmas Eve, or Adam and Eve
**Belly** Darby Kelly
**Bet** House to let
**Bike** Clever Mike or Dirty tyke
**Bill** Jack and Jill, or Beecham pill
*__Bird__** Richard the Third
**Bit of a state** Harry Tate
**Bitter** Apple fritter
**Bloke** Heap of Coke
**Book** Joe Hook
**Boots** Daisy roots
**Booze** River Ouze
**Boozer** Battle cruiser
*__Bottle__** Aristotle
**Bowler** Bottle of Kola
**Box** Darkey Cox
**Boy** San Toy, or Rob Roy
**Braces** Airs and graces
**Brains** Down the drains
**Brandy** Jack the Dandy
**Bread** Uncle Fred

**Breath**  King Death
**Broke**  Hearts of Oak, or Coals and coke
**Brokers**  Engineers and stokers
**Brother**  One and t'other
**Bucket**  Mrs Duckett
*Bug (also Mug)**  Steam tug
**Bus**  Don't make a fuss
**Butter**  Mutter and stutter, or Johnnie Rutter, or Pull down
the shutter

**Cadge**  Coat and badge
**Cake**  Sexton Blake
**Candle**  Harry Randall
**Cash**  Oscar Asche
**Cell**  Flowery dell
**Chair**  Lion's lair
**Cheek**  Once a week
**Cheese**  Stand at ease
*Child (kid)**  Teapot lid, or God forbid
**Church**  Left in the lurch
*Cigarette (fag)**  Oily rag
**Clock**  Dickory dock
**Club (also Pub)**  Rub-a-dub
**Coat**  Quaker oat
**Coffee**  Sticky toffee
**Cold**  Potatoes in the mould, or Cheltenham Bold
**Collar**  Holloa boys holloa
**Copper (cop)**  John Hop
**Corner**  Johnnie Horner
**Crook**  Joe Rook
**Cry**  Pipe your eye
**Cupboard**  Mother Hubbard

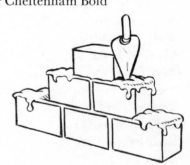

*Daughter**  Bricks and mortar
**Dead**  Brown bread

**Dice** Rats and mice
**Dinner** Jim Skinner
**Dirty** Two-thirty
**Do so** Robinson Crusoe
**Dog** Cherry Hog
*\***Dollar** Oxford scholar
**Door** Rory O'More
**Drawers** Early doors
**Drink** Tumble down the sink
*\***Drunk** Elephant's trunk

**Ear** King Lear
**Egg** Clothes peg
**Evens** Major Stevens
*\***Eye** Mince pie

**Face** Boat Race, or Chevy Chase
**Facts** Brass tacks
**Fare** Grey mare
*\***Feet** Plates of meat
**Fever** Robinson and Cleaver
**Fiddle** Hey diddle diddle
**Fight** Read and write
**Fighter** Typewriter
**Fingers** Longers and lingers
**Fire** Ave Maria, or Obediah, or Jeremiah
**Five** Jack's alive
**Fiver** Lady Godiva
**Flea (also Key)** Jenny Lee
**Flower** Early hour
**Fluke** Iron Duke
**Food** In the nude
**Frock** Almond rock

**Garden** Dolly Varden
**Geezer** Lemon squeezer
*__Gin__ Needle and pin
**Girl** Mother of pearl
**Glass** Khyber Pass, or Hackney Marsh
*__Gloves__ Turtle doves
**Good** Robin Hood
**Gout** Salmon trout, or In and out
**Grass** Ernie Marsh
**Ground** Penny a pound
**Guts** Newington Butts

**Hair** Barnet Fair
**Half a dollar** Half an Oxford scholar
**Hand** German band, or Brass band, or St Martin's-Le-Grand
**Handy** Sugar candy
**Hat** Tit for tat
*__Head__ Uncle Ned, or Lump of lead, or Loaf of bread
**Heart** Raspberry tart, or Jam tart
**Hide** Duck and dive
**Hill** Rhubarb pill
**Home** Gates of Rome
**Horse** Bottle of sauce
**Hot** Peas in the pot
*__House__ Rat and mouse

**Jew** Five to two, or Four by two

**Key** Jenny Lee
*__Kipper__ Jack the Ripper

**Lager** Forsyte Saga
**Legs** Ham and eggs
**Liar** Holy friar, or Dunlop tyre
**Light (ale)** Day and night

**Lodger** Artful Dodger
**Look** Butcher's hook
**Luck** Donald Duck

**Man** Pot and pan
**Match (contest)** Colney Hatch
**Matches** Cuts and scratches
**Mate** China plate
**Mercy** Piccadilly Percy
**Missis (wife)** Cheese and kisses, or Plates and dishes
**Money** Bees and honey
**Morning** Day's dawning, or Gipsy's warning
**Motor** Tea, two and a bloater
**Motor car** Jam jar
**Mouth** North and south
*\***Mug (fool)** Steam tug

**Navy** Soup and gravy
**Neck** Bushel and peck
**Noise** Box of toys
**Nose** I suppose

**Organ** Molly O'Morgan
**Overcoat** I'm afloat
**Own (alone or without aid)** Pat Malone, or Jack Jones, or
Tod Sloan

**Pants** Insects and ants
**Paper** Linen draper
**Park** Light and dark
**Pawn (in—)** Bullock's horn
**Penny (stiver)** Coalheaver or Kilkenny
*\***Phone** Dog and bone
**Piano** Joanna
**Pickle** Harvey Nichol

**Pillow**  Tit willow
**Pinch (steal)**  Half-inch
**Pipe**  Cherry ripe
**Pitch (stall or stand)**  Hedge and ditch
*****Pocket**  Sky rocket
**Pony (£25 or animal)**  Macaroni
**Poof**  Iron hoof
**Pox**  Surrey Docks
**Pub (also Club)**  Rub-a-dub

**Queer**  Brighton Pier, or Ginger beer

**Rain**  Andy Cain
**Rent**  Burton-on-Trent, or Duke of Kent
**Road**  Frog and toad
**Row (quarrel)**  Bull and cow
*****Rum**  Finger and thumb

**Sack (getting the)**  Tin tack
**Sauce**  Rocking horse
**Scotch**  Gold watch
**Scotch (whisky)**  Gay and frisky
**Seas**  Housemaid's knees
**Sense**  Eighteen pence
**Sense (brains)**  Down the drains
**Sex**  Oedipus Rex
**Shabby**  Westminster Abbey
**Shaky**  Currant cakey
**Shave**  Ocean wave, or Dig in the grave
**Shilling**  Thomas Tilling
**Shilling (bob)**  Touch me on the knob
**Shirt**  Dickey Dirt
**Shoe**  How-d'ye-do
**Shop**  Lollipop
**Sick**  Tom and Dick

**Silly** Uncle Willy
**Sixpence (tanner)** Lord of the manor, or Tartan banner
**Sleep (kip)** Bo-peep, or Feather and flip
**Soap** Cape of Good Hope
**Socks** Almond rocks
**Soda** Major Loda
**Son** Bath bun
**Song** Ding dong
**Soup** Loop the loop
**Sovereign** Jimmy O'Goblin
**Sovereign (quid)** Saucepan lid
**Stairs** Apples and pears
**Star** Lah-di-dah
**Steak** Joe Blake
**Steal (pinch)** Half-inch
**Stew** Battle of Waterloo
*\*Stink** Pen and ink
**Suit** Whistle and flute
*\*Sun** Currant bun
**Supper** Tommy Tucker
**Swear** Lord Mayor

**Table** Cain and Abel
**Tailor** Sinbad the Sailor
**Tale** Newgate Gaol
**Talk** Rabbit and pork
**Tap (borrow)** Cellarflap, or Star's nap
**Tart (sweetheart)** Merryheart
**Tea** Rosy Lee, or You and me
**Teeth** Hampstead Heath
**Telly** Ned Kelly
**Ten** Big Ben, or Cock and hen
**Thief** Tea leaf
*\*Tie** Peckham Rye
**Tights** Fly-be-nights

**Time**  Bird lime
**Toast**  Holy Ghost
**Toss**  Iron horse
**Tote**  Canal boat
**Towel**  Mortar and trowel
**Tram**  Baa lamb
**Trousers**  Round the houses
**Tube (underground railway)**  Oxo cube
**Tune**  Stewed prune

**Voice**  Hobson's choice

**Wages**  Rock of Ages, or Greengages
**Waistcoat**  Charlie Prescot
**Waiter**  Hot potato
**Walk**  Ball of chalk
**Watch**  Bottle of Scotch, or Gordon and Gotch
**Water**  Fisherman's daughter
**Week**  Bubble and squeak
**Wife**  Trouble and strife
**Wig**  Irish jig
**Window**  Burnt cinder
**Wishes**  Pots and dishes
**Woman (wife)**  Gooseberry puddin'
**Wood**  Do me good
**Word**  Dicky bird, or Richard the Third

**Yanks**  Sherman tanks

# A cockney's lament

I met a bird one evening
   As I walked down the *frog*.
I'd just come out the *battle*
   And was looking for a *dog*.

She said her name was Julie
   (A single girl, please note).
Her *barnet*, all unruly,
   Hung down across her *boat*.

Her *bristols* pointed at me
   Through a *dicky* crisp and white
Just like a pair of boxing-gloves
   Out looking for a fight.

Her *scotches*, long and slender
   Reached to her *kingdom come*,
Her *hobsons*, low and husky
   Made my *newingtons* go numb.

I took her for some *Lillian Gish*
   Down at the chippy caff.
We squeezed into my *jam-jar*
   And drove back to my gaff.

She then began removing
   Her full-length *almond rock*,
Revealing size nine *how-de-do's*
   Which gave me quite a shock.

And with a sexy *butchers*
    She murmured 'I'm all yours.'
She then took off her *fly-be's*
    And dropped her *early doors*.

Too late I realized it –
    The girl I'd tried to wive
Was an *iron* called Harry Ashcroft
    Who worked for MI5.

# Insults department

Here are a few ethnic examples, just for the record – but I advise strongly against using any of them in mixed company.

| | | | |
|---|---|---|---|
| Dustbin lid | Yid | Silvery moon | Coon |
| Grocer's shop | Wop | Spotty dog | Wog |
| Four by two | Jew | Widow's wink | Chink |
| Jiggle and jog | Frog | Orange pip | Nip |

Who are you calling a *four-by-two*?
You look as if you can't make up your mind whether you're a *spotty* or a *widow's*.

# A sermon in slang

(Given by the Rev McVitie Price, vicar of the church of
St Cain and Abel, Hampstead Heath)

Now many of you here tonight will know that Cain and Abel,
and Hampstead Heath, are cockney rhyming slang. *Cain and
Abel* means table, and *Hampstead Heath* means teeth. We are
glad to welcome tonight a large group of cockney worshippers
to Evensong: and it is to them that I wish to address my
sermon. I want to tell you a story.

A long time ago, in the days of the Israelites, there lived a poor
man. He had no *trouble and strife* – she had run off with a *tea
leaf* some years before – and now he lived with his *bricks and
mortar*, Mary. And being very short of *bees and honey*, and unable
to pay the *Burton-on-Trent*, he was tempted to go forth into the
*Bristol City*, and see what he could *half-inch*. And he would say
to Mary, his *bricks and mortar* – 'I will take a *ball of chalk* into the
town, and buy some tobacco for my *cherry ripe.*'

And he would put on his *almond rocks*, and his *Dicky Dirt*, and
his *round the houses*, and set off down the *frog and toad*, until he
reached the outskirts of the *Bristol*. And people would stare at
him, for his *Dicky Dirt* was torn, his *how-d'ye-do's* were full of holes,
and his coat was *Westminster Abbey*. He was also somewhat
unclean; being too poor to purchase any *Cape of Good Hope*, his
*bushel and peck* was extremely *two-thirty*. And people passed by
on the other side, to avoid the *pen and ink*. He was truly an
ugly man – his *north and south* drooped, his *mince pies* were
watery, and he had a big red *I suppose*.

One day, his *bricks and mortar* gave him some money, saying
'Here is a *saucepan lid* – go and buy food. A loaf of *Uncle Fred*

25

and a pound of *stand-at-ease*. But do not tarry in the town, and
bring me back what is left of the money, to buy myself a new
pair of *early doors*, for my present ones are full of holes, and I
am in a continual *George Raft*.' But instead of returning with the
*bees and honey* for his *bricks and mortar*'s *early doors*, he made his
way to the *rub-a-dub*, for a *tumble down the sink*.

And he became very *elephant's trunk*, and *Mozart*: and when the
landlord of the *rub-a-dub* called *bird lime*, the man set off back
towards his *cat and mouse*, reeling about all over the *frog and
toad*, and drunkenly humming a *stewed prune*. And it came to
*Khyber Pass*, that as he staggered along, he saw, on the
pavement, a small brown *Richard the Third*. And he stared at
it, lying there at his *plates of meat*. And he said, 'Oh small
brown *Richard the Third* – how lucky I did not step on you.'

And he picked it up, and put it on top of a wall, where no one could step on it. And a rich *four-by-two*ish merchant, who witnessed the deed, put his hand into his *sky rocket*, and took out a *Lady Godiva*, and handed it to the man saying, 'I saw you pick up that *Richard the Third* and remove it from the pavement and that was a kindly act. Take this *Lady Godiva* for your *froth and bubble*.' And the man took it and went on his way. And the *Richard the Third* flew back to its nest.

When the man arrived home, his daughter was sitting by the *Jeremiah*, on her favourite *Lionel Blair*.

And the man handed her the money, saying: 'Here is a *Lady Godiva*, which I earned by a kindly act.' And the woman was overjoyed and said, 'Thank you father. Now I can have my pair of *early doors*. Verily, that kindly act has ensured that I have more than enough to cover my *bottle and glass*.'

I thank you all.

# A cross reference
## to the glossary (in alphabetical order)

**Adam and Eve, or Christmas Eve** Believe
**Airs and graces** Braces
**Almond rock** Sock, or Frock
**Andy Cain** Rain
**Apple fritter** Bitter
*__Apples and pears__ Stairs
**Aristotle** Bottle
**Ave Maria, or Obediah, or Jeremiah** Fire

*__Baa lamb__ Tram
**Ball of chalk** Walk
**Barnet Fair** Hair
*__Basin of gravy__ Baby
**Bath bun** Son
**Battle cruiser** Boozer
**Battle of Waterloo** Stew
**Beecham pill, or Jack and Jill** Bill
**Bees and honey** Money
**Beggar boy's ass** Bass
**Big Ben, or Cock and hen** Ten
**Bird lime** Time
**Boat Race** Face
**Bo-peep, or Feather and flip** Sleep (kip)
**Bottle of Kola** Bowler
**Bottle of sauce** Horse
**Bottle of Scotch, or Gordon and Gotch** Watch
**Box of toys** Noise
**Brass tacks** Facts
**Bricks and mortar** Daughter
**Brighton Pier** Queer
**Brown bread** Dead
**Bubble and squeak** Week
**Bull and cow** Row (quarrel)
**Bullock's horn** Pawn (in—)
**Burnt cinder** Window

**Burton-on-Trent, or Duke of Kent** Rent
**Bushel and peck** Neck
**Butcher's hook** Look

**Cain and Abel** Table
**Canal boat** Tote
**Cape of Good Hope** Soap
*__Cat and mouse__ House
**Cellarflap, or Star's nap** Tap (borrow)
**Chalk Farm** Arm
**Charlie Prescot** Waistcoat
*__Cheese and kisses__ Missis
**Cheltenham Bold** Cold
**Cherry Hog** Dog
**Cherry ripe** Pipe
**Chevy Chase** Face
**China plate** Mate
**Christmas Eve, or Adam and Eve** Believe
**Clever Mike** Bike
**Clothes peg** Egg
**Coalheaver, or Kilkenny** Penny
**Coals and coke, or Hearts of Oak** Broke
**Coat and badge** Cadge
**Cock and hen, or Big Ben** Ten
**Cock sparrow** Barrow
**Currant bun** Sun
**Currant cakey** Shaky
**Cuts and scratches** Matches

**Daft and barmy** Army
**Daisy roots** Boots
**Darby Kelly** Belly
**Darky Cox** Box
**Day and night** Light (ale)
**Day's dawning, or Gipsy's warning** Morning

**Derry and Tom** Bomb
**Dickey Dirt** Shirt
**Dickory dock** Clock
**Dicky bird, or Richard the Third** Word
**Dig in the grave, or Ocean wave** Shave
**Ding dong** Song
**Do me good** Wood
**Dog and bone** Phone
*****Donald Duck** Luck
**Down the drains** Brains
**Duck and dive** Hide
**Duke of Kent, or Burton-on-Trent** Rent
**Dunlop tyre, or Holy friar** Liar

**Early doors** Drawers (pair of)
**Early hour** Flower
**Eighteen pence** Sense
**Elephant's trunk** Drunk
**Engineers and stokers** Brokers
**Ernie Marsh** Grass

**Feather and flip, or Bo-peep** Sleep (kip)
**Finger and thumb** Rum
**Fisherman's daughter** Water
**Five to two, or Four by two** Jew
**Flowery dell** Cell
**Fly-be-nights** Tights
**Forsyte Saga** Lager
**Frog and toad** Road

**Gates of Rome** Home
**Gay and frisky** Whisky
**German band, or Brass band, or St Martin's-Le-Grand**
   Hand
**Gertie Gitana** Banana

**Gipsy's warning, or Day's dawning** Morning
**God forbid, or Teapot lid** Child (kid)
**Gold watch** Scotch
**Gooseberry puddin'** Wife (woman)
**Gordon and Gotch, or Bottle of Scotch** Watch
**Greengages, or Rock of Ages** Wages
**Grey mare** Fare

**Hackney Marsh, or Khyber Pass** Glass
**Half an Oxford scholar** Half a dollar
**Half-inch** Pinch (steal)
**Ham and eggs** Legs
**Hampstead Heath** Teeth
**Harry Randall** Candle
**Harry Tate** Bit of a state
**Harvey Nichol** Pickle
**Heap of coke** Bloke
**Hearts of Oak, or Coals and coke** Broke
**Hedge and ditch** Pitch (stall or stand)
**Hey diddle diddle** Fiddle
**Hobson's choice** Voice
**Holloa boys holloa** Collar
**Holy friar, or Dunlop tyre** Liar
**Holy Ghost** Toast
**Hot potato** Waiter
**House to let** Bet
**Housemaid's knee** Sea
**How d'you do** Shoe

**I suppose** Nose
**I'm afloat** Overcoat
**In and out, or Salmon trout** Gout
**In the nude** Food
**Insects and ants** Pants
**Irish jig** Wig

**Iron hoof**  Poof
**Iron horse**  Toss

**Jack and Jill, or Beecham pill**  Bill
**Jack Jones, or Tod Sloan, or Pat Malone**  Own (alone)
**Jack the Dandy**  Brandy
**Jack the Ripper**  Kipper
**Jack's alive**  Five
*****Jam jar**  Car
*****Jam tart, or Raspberry tart**  Heart
**Jenny Lee**  Flea, or Key
**Jeremiah, or Ave Maria, or Obediah**  Fire
**Jimmy O'Goblin**  Sovereign
**Jim Skinner**  Dinner
**Joanna**  Piano
**Joe Hook**  Book
**Joe Rook**  Crook
**John Hop**  Cop (policeman)
**Johnnie Horner**  Corner
**Johnnie Rutter, or Mutter and stutter**  Butter
**Jumping Jack**  Back

**Khyber Pass, or Hackney Marsh**  Glass
**Kilkenny, or Coalheaver (from stiver)**  Penny
*****King Death**  Breath
**King Lear**  Ear

**Lah-di-dah**  Star
*****Lady Godiva**  Fiver
**Left in the lurch**  Church
**Lemon squeezer**  Geezer
**Light and dark**  Park
**Lillian Gish**  Fish
**Linen draper**  Paper
**Lion's lair**  Chair

**Loaf of bread, or Uncle Ned, or Lump of lead** Head
**Lodger** Artful Dodger
**Lollipop** Shop
**Longers and lingers** Fingers
**Loop the loop** Soup
**Lord of the manor, or Tartan banner** Tanner (sixpence)
**Lord Mayor** Swear
**Lump of lead, or Uncle Ned, or Loaf of bread** Head

**Macaroni**  Pony (£25, or animal)
**Major Loda**  Soda
**Major Stevens**  Evens (betting)
**Me and you**  Menu
**Merryheart**  Tart (sweetheart)
**Mince pie**  Eye
**Molly O'Morgan**  Organ
**Mortar and trowel**  Towel
**Mother Hubbard**  Cupboard
**Mother of pearl**  Girl
**Mrs Chant**  Aunt
**Mrs Duckett**  Bucket
**Mutter and stutter, or
  Johnnie Rutter**  Butter

*Ned Kelly**  Telly
**Needle and pin**  Gin
**Newgate Gaol**  Tale
**Newington Butts**  Guts
**North and south**  Mouth

**Obediah, or Ave Maria, or
  Jeremiah**  Fire
**Ocean wave, or
  Dig in the grave**  Shave
**Oedipus Rex**  Sex
*Oily rag**  Fag
**Once a week**  Cheek
**One and t'other**  Brother
**Oscar Asche**  Cash
**Oxford scholar**  Dollar
**Oxo cube**  Tube
  (underground railway)

**Pat Malone, or Jack Jones, or Tod Sloan** Own (alone)
*Peas in the pot** Hot
**Peckham Rye** Tie
**Pen and ink** Stink
**Penny a pound** Ground
**Piccadilly Percy** Mercy
**Pig's ear** Beer
**Pipe your eye** Cry
**Plates and dishes** Missis
**Plates of meat** Feet
**Pot and pan** Man
**Potatoes in the mould, or Cheltenham Bold** Cold
**Pots and dishes** Wishes
**Pull down the shutter, or Mutter and stutter, etc** Butter

**Quaker oat** Coat

**Rabbit and pork** Talk
**Raspberry tart, or Jam tart** Heart
**Rat and mouse** House
**Rats and mice** Dice
**Read and write** Fight
*Reels of cotton** Rotten
**Rhubarb pill** Hill
**Richard the Third** Word, or Bird
**River Ouze** Booze
**Rob Roy, or San Toy** Boy
**Robin Hood** Good
**Robinson Crusoe** Do so
**Robinson and Cleaver** Fever
**Rock of Ages, or Greengages** Wages
*Rocking horse** Sauce
**Rory O'More** Door
**Rosy Lee, or You and me** Tea
**Round the houses** Trousers
**Rub-a-dub** Pub (or Club)

**St Martin's-Le-Grand, or Brass band, or German band**
    Hand
**Salmon trout, or In and out**  Gout
**San Toy, or Rob Roy**  Boy
\***Saucepan lid**  Quid
**Scotch peg**  Egg
**Sexton Blake**  Cake
**Shepherd's plaid, or Sorry and sad**  Bad
**Sherman tanks**  Yanks
**Sinbad the Sailor**  Tailor
**Skein of thread**  Bed
**Skin and blister**  Sister
**Sky rocket**  Pocket
**Sorry and sad, or Shepherd's plaid**  Bad
**Soup and gravy**  Navy
**Stand at ease**  Cheese
**Star's nap, or Cellarflap**  Tap (borrow)
**Steam tug**  Mug (fool)
**Stewed prune**  Tune
\***Sticky toffee**  Coffee
**Stop thief**  Beef
**Sugar candy**  Handy
**Surrey Docks**  Pox

**Tartan banner, or Lord of the manor**  Tanner (sixpence)
**Tea leaf**  Thief
**Teapot lid, or God forbid**  Kid (child)
**Tea, two, and a bloater**  Motor
**Thomas Tilling**  Shilling
**Tin tack**  Sack
**Tin tank**  Bank
**Tit for tat**  Hat
**Tit willow**  Pillow
**Tod Sloan, or Jack Jones, or Pat Malone**  Own (alone)
**Tom and Dick**  Sick

**Tommy Tucker** Supper
**Touch me on the knob** Bob (shilling)
**Trouble and strife** Wife
**Tumble down the sink** Drink
**Turtle doves** Gloves
**Two-thirty** Dirty
**Typewriter** Fighter

**Uncle Fred** Bread
**Uncle Ned, or Loaf of bread, or Lump of lead** Head
**Uncle Willy** Silly

**Westminster Abbey** Shabby
**Whistle and flute** Suit

**You and me, or Rosy Lee** Tea

# The Queen's Christmas Speech to the Nation

(translated into rhyming slang)

My *old Dutch* and I, as we sit by our *Jeremiah* in Buckingham Palace, with our *Gawd fer bids* by our side, are especially thinking of you all this Christmas Tide; sitting in your own *rat and mouse*, clustered round the *Ned Kelly*, or having a bit of a *ding-dong* round the old *Joanna*. How I wish we could be with you all today, sharing a pint of *pig's ear*, or filling our *Darbies* round your *Cain and Abel*. But this cannot be.

I greet, too, the Empire, upon which the *currant bun* never sets. Whether you are in the *daft and barmy* maintaining law and order in a far flung outpost, or in the Royal *Soup and gravy*, afloat on the high *housemaid's knees*, I greet you all, with my warmest *pots and dishes*.

As we take a *butcher's hook* at what lies before us on the *frog and toad* ahead, let us remember those less fortunate than ourselves: those who are on their *Jack Jones*; a man without a *tit willow* to lay his head on; a girl, very much down on her *Donald Duck*; those who are *taters in the mould*; those without any *in the nude* at all; and let us be thankful for small *Piccadilly Percys*.

Now I must leave you, as Philip has just rolled in from the *rub-a-dub*, and is in a right old *two-and-eight*, thinking he has missed his *Jim Skinner*, so I will have to go and pour him a large *Forsyte Saga* to keep him quiet. Therefore, in conclusion, may I wish you a happy New Year. My *jam tart* goes with you all.

# A few lah-di's

Being some of the famous faces who
have lent their names to the slang.

(lah-di-dah = star)

Vera Lynn – Gin

Lionel Blair – Chair

Gregory Peck – Neck

George Raft – Draught

Errol Flynn – Chin

Clark Gable – Table

J. Carroll Naish – Slash

Lillian Gish – Fish

# Puzzle page

TOM TIT

NOOK AND CRANNY

ORCHESTRA STALLS

MOZART AND LISZT

KHYBER PASS

BRISTOL CITIES

BOTTLE AND GLASS

FILLET OF COD

KINGDOM COME

*The Clues* (a piece of narrative from a Covent Garden porter)

'I'd just been into the bog for a *Tom Tit*, its the only place you can sit and read the paper in peace round here. Well, on the way back, I slipped on a banana skin and fell flat on me *nook and cranny*. I was lucky I didn't damage me *orchestra stalls*. Of course, everybody thought I was *Mozart and Liszt*, falling flat on my *Khyber Pass* like that. Some girl went past, with an upturned nose and *Bristol Cities* to match.

'"Fallen on your *bottle and glass*, have you? Hope you haven't damaged your brains," she said. Cheeky little *fillet of cod*. What she needed was a good smack on the *Kingdom come*.'

Some of the more indelicate ones are listed opposite – but the translations are left to your own imagination.

# Fashion section
(a quick and handy reference to the male attire)

| Daisies | Daisy roots | Boots |
|---------|-------------|-------|
| Almonds | Almond rocks | Socks |
| Dicky | Dicky Dirt | Shirt |
| Oxford | Oxford scholar | Collar |
| Peckham | Peckham Rye | Tie |
| Quaker | Quaker oat | Coat |
| Rounds | Round the houses | Trousers |
| Titfer | Titfer tat | Hat |
| Sky | Sky rocket | Pocket |

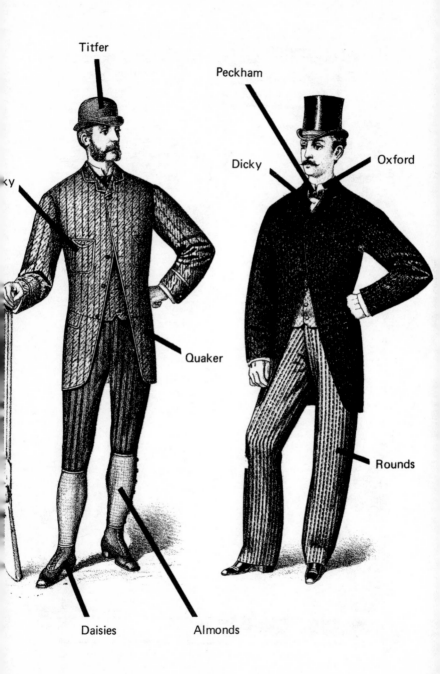

Titfer

Peckham

Dicky

Oxford

ky

Quaker

Rounds

Daisies

Almonds

# A cockney menu

### *Starters*
Loop
or
Lillian

### *Main course*
Roast Stop
Darby of Pork
Braised Down the Drains
Irish Battle

Gerties and Cream
or
Stand at Ease

Sticky or Rosie

### *Note*
All meals served with Uncle Fred
and Johnnie Rutter

If you can't decipher the menu opposite, here are a few picture clues. (And a red herring.)

Red Herring

Ronnie Barker was born in Bedford in 1929. He studied architecture before turning to the theatre. Early work in repertory theatre was followed by increasing success on television – first with *The Ronnie Barker Playhouse* and *Frost on Sunday* and then with Ronnie Corbett in *The Two Ronnies*.

He is now most closely associated with the character of Fletcher, lag extraordinary, in three series of *Porridge* and one *Going Straight*. Fletcher is back behind bars once more for the film version of *Porridge*.

Ronnie Barker already has a number of feature film appearances to his credit. He has produced a number of successful comedy books – *The Ronnie Barker Book of Bathing Beauties*, *The Ronnie Barker Book of Boudoir Beauties*, *It's Goodnight from Him*, *Sauce* and now *Fletcher's Book of Rhyming Slang*.

Ronnie Barker is married with one daughter and two sons.

. . . and I bet a Monkey you *still* don't know
what I'm talking about, do you? Ta-ta!